1. MiG-23ML (Flogger-G)

2. Tu-22M-3 (Backfire-C)

SOVIET WINGS

Modern Soviet Military Aircraft

Alexander M. Dzhus

Edited and introduced by John W. R. Taylor
Editor Emeritus, *Jane's All the World's Aircraft*

Greenhill Books, London
Presidio Press, California

Soviet Wings first published 1991 by Greenhill Books,
Lionel Leventhal Limited, Park House, 1 Russell Gardens,
London NW11 9NN
and
Presidio Press, 31 Pamaron Way, Novato, Ca.94949, U.S.A.

Photographs © Alexander M. Dzhus, 1991
Introduction and Aircraft Specifications © John W. R. Taylor, 1991
3-view drawings © Pilot Press
Collective work © Lionel Leventhal Limited, 1991, Park House,
1 Russell Gardens, London NW11 9NN
Soviet Wings has been created by Lionel Leventhal Limited in
association with Planeta Publishers, Moscow

British Library Cataloging in Publication Data
Dzhus, Alexander M.
Soviet wings: modern Soviet military aircraft.
1. Soviet military forces. Military aircraft
I. Title II. Taylor, John W. R. (John William Ransom) *1922–*
623.7460947
ISBN 1-85367-094-4

Library of Congress Cataloging-in-Publication Data
Dzhus, Alexander M.
Soviet wings: modern military Soviet aircraft/by Alexander M.
Dzhus; edited by John W. R. Taylor.
192p. 30cm.

ISBN 1-85367-094-4: $50.00
1. Airplanes, Military—Soviet Union. I. Taylor, John William Ransom.
II. Title.
UG1245.S65D94 1991
358.4'183'0947—dc20

Quality printing and binding by Colorcraft Ltd, 6A, Victoria Centre,
15 Watson's Road, North Point, Hong Kong.

Designed by DAG Publications Ltd

Acknowledgements I would like to thank the pilots whose expert
airmanship helped to make this project possible. They are: Ya.
Alpatyev, A. Arestov, V. Bazhenov, V. Basov, S. Bezlyudny, A.
Bokach, V. Bukin, V. Burukin, V. Bychkov, V. Vazhinsky, A. Verozub,
S. Ganichev, B. Grigoryev, A. Dyatlov, R. Kaliyev, I. Kirsanov, V.
Kravets, V. Kravtsov, A. Kutuzov, A. Lichkun, A. Petrov, N. Rozhkov,
I. Sakhnenko, A. Spitsa, V. Solovyov, V. Tikhenko, V. Shilin, N.
Chaga and V. Yashin.
 I wish to express my appreciation to Colonel-General of the Air
Forces S. Golubev, Colonel-General of the Air Forces I. Dmitriyev,
Colonel-General of the Air Forces P. Deinekin, Major-General of
the Air Forces G. Laptev, Major-General of the Air Forces V.
Longvinenko and Colonel V. Ivanov for their invaluable help in
arranging the flights.
 Finally my thanks to A. Tarasova and G. Drugoveiko.

Alexander Dzhus

Contents

Introduction

by John W. R. Taylor

Never before has there been a book like this . . . Since the world's first successful four-engined aeroplane was designed and built by Igor Sikorsky at St Petersburg (now Leningrad), and flown by him on 13 May 1913, Soviet engineers have produced a succession of remarkable aircraft. Sadly, they have seldom been illustrated adequately. Even in the years following World War II, when advances in air-to-air photography in the West kept pace with the transformation from piston-engined aeroplanes to swept-wing jets, there appeared to be no parallel improvement in the standard of illustrations in the East.

Nobody doubted the capability of the men responsible for the MiGs, Tupolevs and Ilyushins known to be in air force service. The only available photographs, often heavily retouched, led one exasperated journalist to complain that 'They must build their aeroplanes blurred'.

Glasnost has changed all that. As this book demonstrates, there is a new generation of aerial photographers in the Soviet Union as highly skilled in their profession as the men and women whose products they capture on colour film. Nor is there any longer a severe restriction on their subjects. People buying this example of the work of Alexander Dzhus will not need to search for the superstars among a huge crowd of extras. Twenty-year-old types like the MiG-21, Su-15 and Yak-28 might still serve with units of the Soviet air forces in less critical areas. In this book, the very latest bombers, fighters and attack aircraft are portrayed on most pages.

The majority are shown in their natural element, the air, rather than static and lifeless on an airfield or in a factory. Some photographs were taken from a two-seat aeroplane, in formation with others, during a loop at high speed. Readers of *Soviet Wings*, except for pilots and professional air photographers, may not appreciate the difficulty of obtaining sharp, well-framed, pictures while the visual world is spinning and every part of one's body, as well as the camera, is being wrenched by 'g' forces at several times its natural weight. None will dismiss the banks of white clouds, the sun – sometimes blinding, sometimes blood-red – and the distant downward glimpses of landscapes, as insignificant features of the flier's world.

It will never be possible to relish good photographs of that four-engined Sikorsky of 1913; but we know that, without it, there would have been no Ilya Mourometz four-engined bombers in the 'Squadron of Flying Ships' (EVK) in 1914–18. Nor might there have been, in a book like this, pictures of the mighty Tu-160, the largest and one of the fastest strategic bombers in the modern world. The Tu-160's own immediate predecessors, such as the Tu-22M and Tu-95/142, and the West's B-52s and Vulcans, have played a key role in maintaining peace, through a worldwide fear of mutual annihilation, during four of the most hazardous decades in world history, now ended.

Today, the bombers of East and West, and their human aircrew, symbolize a united determination to utilize air power in the cause of peace and justice, far more convincingly than any impersonal missiles concealed in underground silos . . . But this is a book about aeroplanes, not military philosophy or politics.

Like many of the more advanced modern military aircraft, the Tu-160 uses variable-geometry (swing) wings to combine the advantages of traditional and modern aerodynamics. For take-off, its wings are locked in a forward position, swept back at only 20°, to give a huge span that lifts the 275-tonne bomber quickly into the air with its load of twelve air-launched cruise missiles, twenty-four short-range attack missiles or other weapons. For cruising flight, at almost twice the speed of sound at high altitude, the wings are swept back at 65°.

Although some 20 per cent longer than its US counterpart, the B-1B Lancer, it can fly much faster and farther. On 15 May 1990 the fourteenth Tu-160 flew around a 1,000km (621-mile) course at 1,068mph (1,720km/h), carrying a load of 30,000kg (66,137lb). In doing so, it set nine international records.

One of its four Type 'R' engines, giving 55,115lb (245kN) of thrust, was installed in a canister under the belly of a four-turboprop Tu-142 for testing in flight. On 9 May 1990 this aircraft (known as the Tu-142LL – flying laboratory) also set a series of records. Using its five engines, it climbed to a height of 6,000m (19,685ft) in 4 minutes 23 seconds, and to 9,000m (29,527ft) in 6 minutes 3.5 seconds. It then maintained a height of 12,500m (41,010ft) in horizontal flight.

These were no more than the latest incidents in the story of a remarkable aircraft. Back in 1950, the Soviet long-range aviation force needed a medium-range bomber in the class of the US Air Force's B-47 Stratojet and an intercontinental bomber to match the eight-jet B-52 Stratofortress, then under development. Early examples of Andrei Tupolev's proposals to meet these requirements, the Tu-16 and Tu-95, were exhibited in the sky over Moscow during the 1954 and 1955 Aviation Day flypasts respectively.

Nobody doubted that the twin-jet Tu-16 would enter large-scale production. Some 2,000 were delivered eventually to the Soviet air forces and naval aviation units, in the immense variety of forms listed in the aircraft specifications section of this book. Only the flight-refuelling version is illustrated, as manufacture of the Tu-16 has long ended in the Soviet Union. The Tu-95 is different.

When it first appeared, more than 35 years ago, most students of air power in the West saw little future for what seemed to be a typically Soviet huge, lumbering, turboprop-powered aircraft, and expected it to be abandoned in favour of Myasishchev's four-jet bomber, known to NATO as 'Bison', which had been developed simultaneously. It was believed that the propellers of a turboprop aircraft limited it to speeds far below those of comparable jets, and that all such a powerplant had to offer was better fuel economy. Opinions changed when Tu-95s began to set world records 100mph (160km/h) higher than anyone had expected, and displayed such astonishing range that the Soviet air forces had no hesitation in preferring it to the Myasishchev jet.

About 200 'Bisons' were built, most of which were modified later for maritime reconnaissance, and for in-flight refuelling when the Soviet air forces recognized the value of this method of extending the range of their bomber force. Initially, they devised a unique system of transferring fuel from one Tu-16 to another by the wingtip-to-wingtip technique shown in plate 117 of this book. Much better is the probe-and-drogue method pioneered by the British Flight Refuelling company, and this was copied for the M-3 'Bison' tanker, which is still in service but is being replaced steadily by the Il-78 that can refuel three aircraft at a time, again using a system first demonstrated by Flight Refuelling Ltd.

Meanwhile, the Tu-95 has, through the years, shown itself capable of carrying extensive avionics and the largest air-to-surface missiles and radars fitted to any combat aircraft. It took on new missions over land and sea, proving so adaptable that it was worthwhile for the Tupolev OKB (design bureau) to undertake a major redesign of the airframe, with a new wing and length-ened fuselage, to produce the Tu-142 version. So it became the only combat aircraft ever to remain in continuous production for more than 35 years, and now carries air-launched cruise missiles on an advanced rotary launcher, just like new bombers of the 1980s and '90s.

The achievements of the Tupolev OKB's bomber design teams have been well matched by those of Soviet engineers responsible for transport aircraft and helicopters, and by the Mikoyan and Sukhoi fighter OKBs. It may be true to suggest that Soviet industry could not equal the best products of Western tech-nology until the advent of the current MiG-29 and Su-27, but the merits of simple, easily maintained airframes should never be overlooked. In particular, the MiG-21, with a wing span smaller than that of the tiny Gnats that once equipped the Royal Air Force's 'Red Arrows' aerobatic team, could be flown and kept serviceable by small third world air forces.

The influence of the MiG-15, patriarch of the modern Mikoyan jet family, is clear in a 1986 bulletin from GIFAS, the French aerospace industries association. It states that:

'During the Korean War, the West was very impressed by the Soviet MiG-15, employed in great numbers. French Air Force Headquarters showed much interest in the simplicity and sturdiness of this fighter, which was a good performer and carried a heavy weapon load. As early as 1952, the French Ministry of Armament issued a call for bids for a small aircraft capable of climbing to 18,000 metres in six minutes. During this period, the other Western powers were pursuing similar objectives, which led to the creation of such aircraft as Folland's Gnat in Britain, Italy's Fiat G-91 and the Douglas A-4 Skyhawk in the USA.'

The French response was the Mirage, embodying what the West considered to be the Soviet philosophy of 'Make it simple, make it strong, but make it work'.

In a modern combat environment, the MiG-29 and Su-27 can no longer be as simple as their predecessors, but they are second to none in performance and fighting ability. Their equipment includes an infra-red search/track sensor, which enables an enemy aircraft to be located and attacked by detecting heat emitted by its engines or by the leading-edge of its wings in high-speed flight. The Soviet fighters need emit no radar signals that would warn the enemy of their presence, and could complete their attack before their approach was suspected. Western air forces, which once fitted infra-red sensors to their fighters, feel that they can no longer afford them. Yet, surely, this offers a degree of 'stealth' in combat that might be as effective as the techniques being built into America's new ATF 'stealth' fighters at immense cost in money, complexity and serviceability.

Today, the once-vital quest for air superiority on each side of an Iron Curtain in Europe has passed. Air force leaders of East and West fly in each other's aircraft. Soviet fighters capture the headlines at air shows in Paris, Farnborough and North America. To haul outsize loads across intercontinental distances, companies from Australia, Western Europe and Canada charter Antonov An-124 transports, which maintain the 78-year-old Russian/Soviet tradition of building the 'world's biggest'. And this book has become possible.

Alexander M. Dzhus

I first met Alexander Dzhus in Transbaikalia about fifteen years ago, when I was commander of the forces in the region. One day a tall, handsome man with a camera in his hands burst into my office and said: 'I want to take pictures of combat aircraft in flight, and you must help me.'

The situation was very complicated because at that time the older Soviet aerial photography experts were no longer flying and the link between the art of photography and military aviation had been broken – a real loss, I thought. In those days to restore such a link would be difficult; nevertheless, I retained a desire to share the wonders of aviation with my fellow countrymen.

I listened to the audacious photographer and could see that he would not give up, which is why I decided to help him get flight clearance. Even with my authority as local commander, it still took a lot of time and energy (and I had to be very diplomatic) to obtain authorization for Alexander Dzhus to fly in combat aircraft. These efforts I have never regretted: my young friend not only regenerated aviation photography but surpassed in skill the photographers of the past. Today several photographers 'work in the air', but there is no doubt that Alexander Dzhus is the best of them. Time and again he comes up with new subjects for, and approaches to, aviation photography; while his work remains consis-

tently interesting for its depth of psychological perception.

Practically any work by Dzhus is a unique piece of photographic art. But who can tell the difficulties he faces in order to realize his conceptions? While he may seem to be taking pictures of aircraft, he is in fact taking pictures of pilots. It takes him a long time to find his main characters. It is far from a question of simply taking pictures: he lives in military garrisons for months, getting acquainted with the pilots and exchanging ideas with them. Only then do they take off together. So, when he is in flight, he is with friends. In the air, pilots and photographer understand each other without any problem. They are members of a team creating a picture, united in a desire to catch the best moment of the flight.

In this book you will find photographs taken during the last few years. In fact, they are the result of fifteen years' of Alexander Dzhus 'living' military aviation. I hope that the reader of this book will not only see beautiful pictures but will also find something for his soul.

Colonel-General of the Air Forces (Retired)
IGOR DMITRIYEV, President of the Russian Innovation Association ROSINTRANS.

Born in Khabarovsk, a city in the Soviet Far East, Alexander Dzhus returned to the region for the first time in many years recently when his reporting took him there from Moscow. For thirty years he had lived in nearby areas: in Kurgan, a city in Siberia, and Chita in the Baikal region. His ancestors were Baikal Kazakhs, who several centuries ago settled in this austere and far-away land.

When Alexander was fifteen, his father died. This forced the boy to get a job at a factory and in this way share responsibility for the welfare of the family with his mother. Later he served in the army for two years, graduating from secondary school by correspondence before choosing the career that he has pursued to this day – photography. It took him several years to work out the unique style of reporting that best reflects his personality. It is not in his nature to like large, quietly flowing rivers; he prefers mountain rapids

and waterfalls. So it is not surprising that he has made military aviation the main topic of his attention.

He took his first photographs from on board a jet fighter in the Baikal region some ten years ago. Persistent, perhaps even stubborn, in his desire to do an unusual job, he managed to overcome all obstacles

and make his dream come true: the Air Force Command gave its approval, a doctor gave him a check-up, and he was taken on his first flight. From this he brought back a photo-, graph that was eventually to be accepted by the All-Union Photo Exhibition and was included in one of the books featuring the best photographs of the year. Several years later Dzhus moved to Moscow to work for *Aviatsia & Kosmonavtika* (Aviation & Cosmonautics) magazine.

Alexander Dzhus is 37 years old. He has a long-standing relationship with Planeta Publishers, who are currently producing two books by him, *Aral, the Face of Catastrophe* and *Forever Alive*, which concerns the life and creative activity of the Russian Poetess Anna Akhmatova.

His interests in photography are diverse and, as in the past, among his best friends are the pilots who helped him to produce his unique photographs.

5. MiG-23 (Flogger)

7. MiG-23MF (Flogger-B)

6. MiG-23 (Flogger)

8. MiG-23ML (Flogger-G)

9. MiG-23ML (Flogger-G)

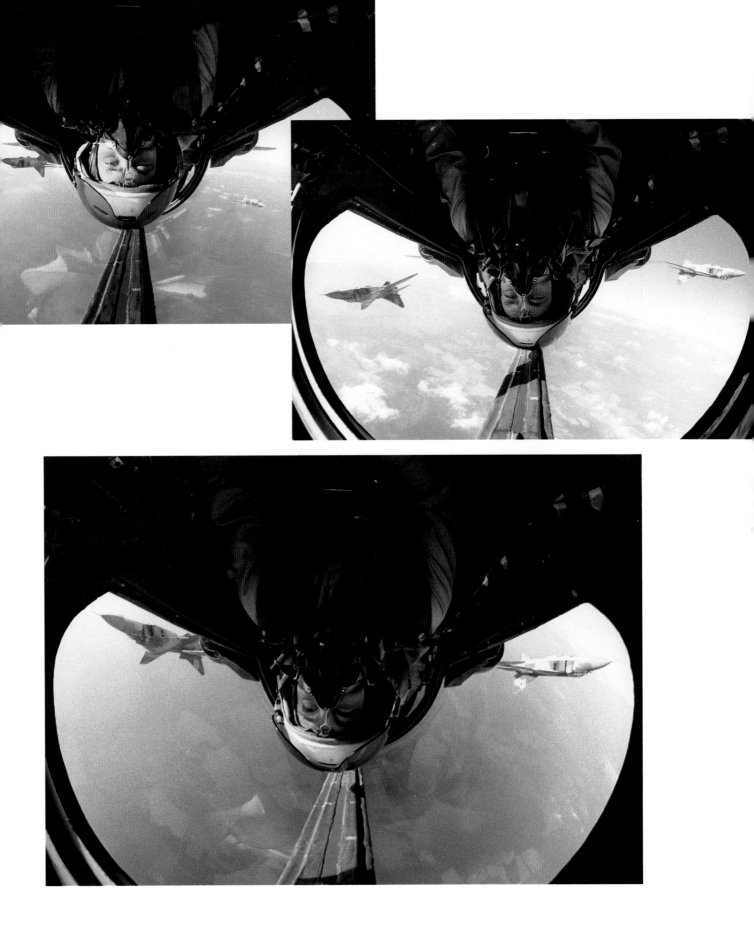

16. MiG-25R (Foxbat-D)

17–19. MiG-25
(Foxbat)

20. MiG-25 (Foxbat)

22. MiG-29 (Fulcrum)

23. MiG-29 (Fulcrum-A)

24. MiG-29 (Fulcrum-A)

25. MiG-29 (Fulcrum-C)

26. MiG-29 (Fulcrum-A)

27–29. MiG-29 (Fulcrum-A)

31–33. MiG-29 (Fulcrum-A)

35. MiG-29 (Fulcrum-A)   36. MiG-29s, Tu-160, Il-78 & Mi-26 (Fulcrum-A, Blackjack, Midas & Halo)

37. MiG-29 (Fulcrum-A)

39. MiG-29 (Fulcrum-A)

40. MiG-29 (Fulcrum-A)

41–43. MiG-29 (Fulcrum-A)

44-45. MiG-29 (Fulcrum-A)   46. MiG-29 (Fulcrum-B)

47. MiG-29 (Fulcrum-A)

48–49. MiG-29 (Fulcrum-A)

50. MiG-29 (Fulcrum-A)

51. Su-17M-4 (Fitter-K)

52. Su-17 (Fitter-C)

53. Su-17 (Fitter)

54–55. Su-17 (Fitter)

56. Su-17M-4 (Fitter-K)

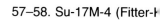

59. Su-17 (Fitter)

60. Su-17 (Fitter-C)

63. Su-17M-4 (Fitter-K)

64. Su-24MK (Fencer-D)

65. Su-25K (Frogfoot-A)

66. Su-25K (Frogfoot-A)

67–69. Su-25K (Frogfoot-A)

70. Su-25K (Frogfoot-A)

71. Su-27 (Flanker-B)

72. Su-27 (Flanker-B)

73. Su-27 (Flanker-B)

74–75. Su-27 (Flanker-B)

77–78. Su-27 (Flanker-B)

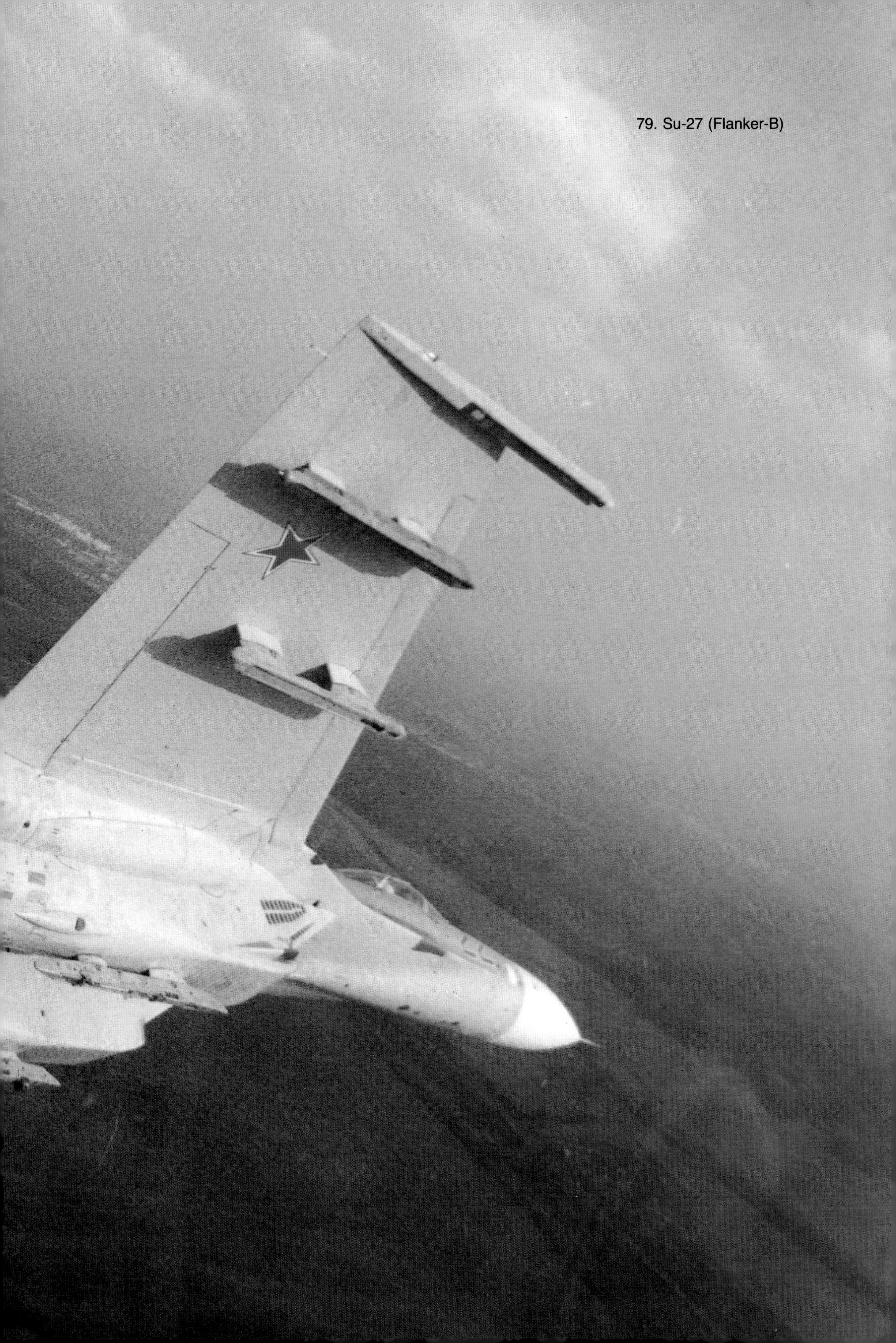

79. Su-27 (Flanker-B)

80–81. Su-27 (Flanker-B)

82. *Tbilisi*

83. Su-27 (Flanker-D)

84–86. Su-27 (Flanker-D)

87–88. Su-27 (Flanker-D)

89–90. Su-27 (Flanker-D)

91–92. Yak-38 (Forger-A)

93–94. Tu-22 (Blinder-B)

95–97. Tu-22 (Blinder-B)

98. Tu-22M-2 (Backfire-B)

99–100. Tu-22M-2 (Backfire-B)

101. Tu-95 (Bear-G)

102–103. Tu-95 (Bear)

104. Tu-95 (Bear)

105. Tu-142 (Bear-H)

106. Tu-160 (Blackjack-A)

107. Tu-160 (Blackjack-A)

108–111. Tu-160 (Blackjack-A)

112. Tu-160 (Blackjack-A)

113. Tu-160 (Blackjack-A)

114. Tu-160 (Blackjack-A)

115–116. Tu-160
(Blackjack-A)

117. Tu-16R (Badger-F)

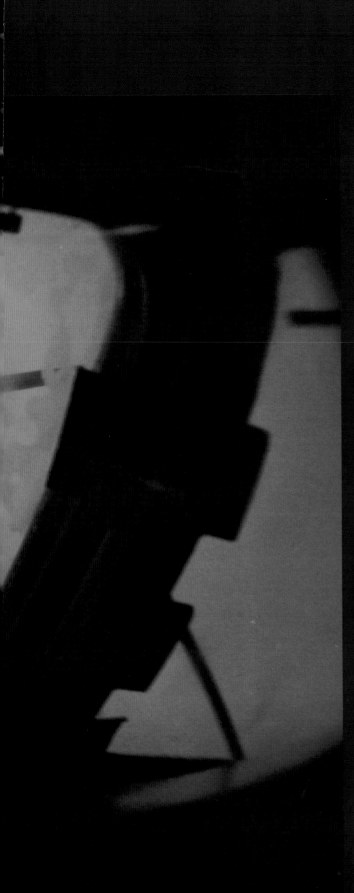

118. M-3 (Bison) & Tu-95 (Bear)
119. M-3 (Bison)

120. Il-78 (Midas)
& Tu-95 (Bear)

121–122. An-124 (Condor)

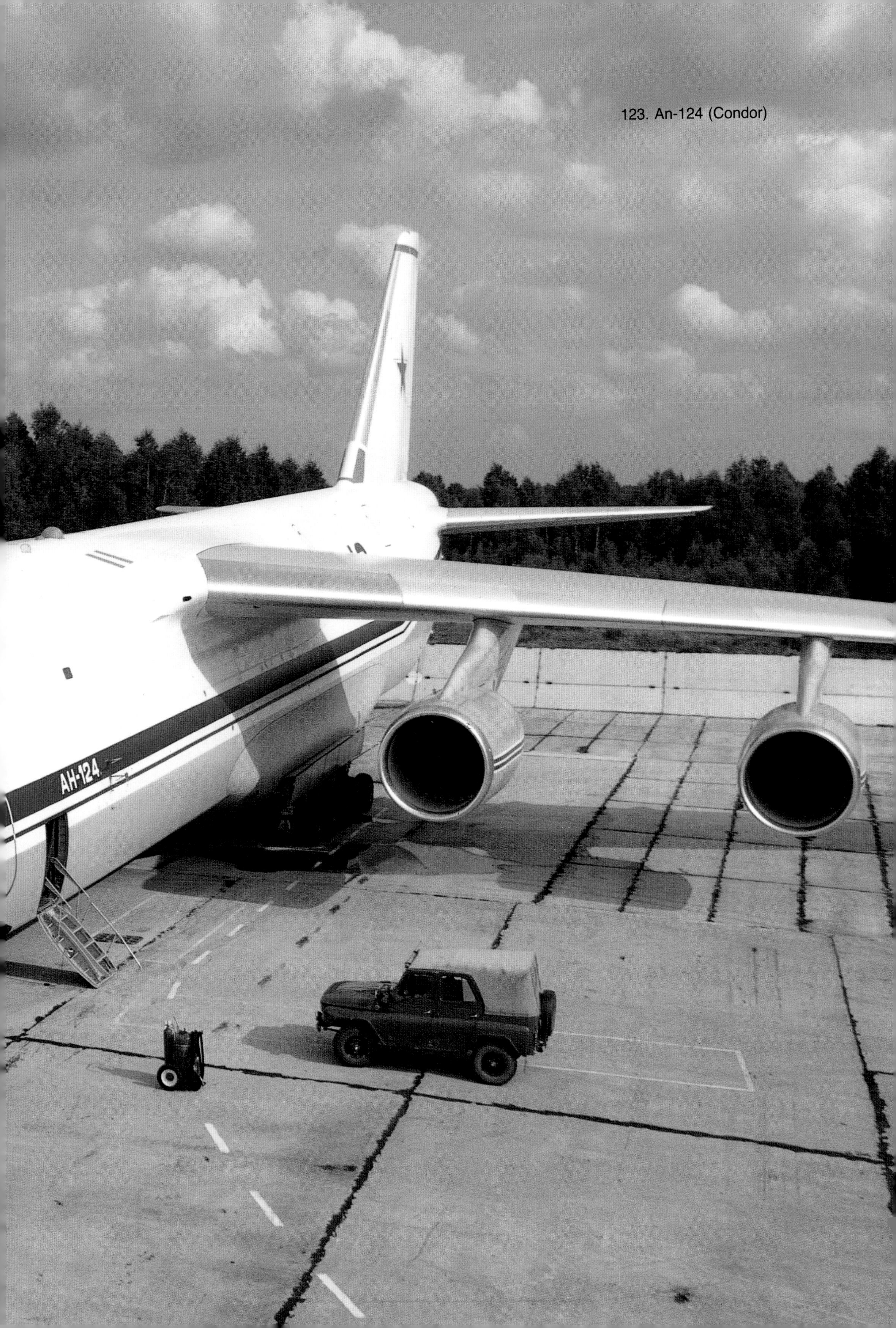

123. An-124 (Condor)

125. An-22 (Cock)

124. An-124 (Condor)

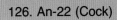

127. An-12 (Cub-C)

130. Il-76MD (Candid-B)

131. Mi-8TBK (Hip-E)

132. Mi-8 (Hip)

133. Mi-8 (Hip)

135–136. Mi-24W (Hind-E)

137. Mi-24W (Hind-E) &
Mi-24 (Hind-G)

138. Mi-26 (Halo)

139. Ka-25BSh (Hormone-A) & Be-12 (Mail)

140. Be-12 (Mail)

141. Be-12 (Mail)

Aircraft Specifications

MIKOYAN MiG-23

NATO Reporting Name: 'Flogger'
Air combat fighter, with variable-geometry wings
First flight: 1967
Estimated number operational in Soviet air forces: 1,800

Variants

'Flogger-B' (MiG-23MF). Single-seat fighter with Tumansky R-29B turbojet, rated at 27,500lb (122kN) thrust with afterburning. J band radar ('High Lark' to NATO). First Soviet fighter with demonstrated ability to destroy targets flying below its own altitude. Entered service about 1975 to supersede original MiG-23M.
'Flogger-C' (MiG-23UM). Tandem two-seat combat-capable trainer with Tumansky R-27 afterburning turbojet, rated at 22,485lb (100kN) thrust.
'Flogger-G' (MiG-23ML). 'L' of designation identifies this lightened version of MiG-23MF, with smaller dorsal fin, rear fuselage fuel tank deleted, lightweight radar and R-35F engine. First seen in 1978.
'Flogger-H' (MiG-23BN). Ground-attack fighter with nose of MiG-27 ('Flogger-D') and MiG-23 power-plant and gun.
'Flogger-K' (MiG-23MLD). Development of MiG-23ML with smaller ventral folding fin, notch at each junction of fixed inboard wing leading-edge and air intake duct, new IFF, pivoting weapon pylons under outer wings, and AA-11 ('Archer') missiles on fuselage pylons.

Data for 'Flogger-G'

Engine: Tumansky R-35F-300 turbojet, rated at 28,660lb (127.5kN) thrust with afterburning.
Wing span: 45ft 10in (13.965m) with wings spread; 25ft 6¼in (7.779m) with wings swept
Length excluding nose probe: 52ft 1¼in (15.88m)
Height: 15ft 9¾in (4.82m)
Maximum take-off weight: 32,625–39,250lb (14,800–17,800kg)
Maximum level speed: Mach 2.35 (1,550mph; 2,500km/h) at height; Mach 1.15 (875mph; 1,405km/h) at sea-level
Operational ceiling: 59,055ft (18,000m)
Combat radius: 715 miles (1,150km) with six air-to-air missiles; 435 miles (700km) with 4,410lb (2,000kg) of bombs
Operational Equipment and Armament: J band multi-mode radar ('High Lark 2'). Infra-red sensor, radar warning system and chaff/flare dispensers. One 23mm twin-barrel gun under fuselage. Typical interception armament of two medium-range semi-active radar homing AA-7 ('Apex') and four AA-8 ('Aphid') close-range infra-red missiles. Provision for 6,615lb (3,000kg) of bombs, rockets and other weapons in ground-attack role.

Picture notes

9. MiG-23s in diamond formation, at sunset.
10–15. Formation of MiG-23s photographed during a loop.

MIKOYAN MiG-25

NATO Reporting Name: 'Foxbat'
The world's fastest combat aircraft, used by interceptor and reconnaissance units
First flight: about 1964
Estimated number operational in Soviet air forces: 550

Variants

'Foxbat-B and D' (MiG-25R). Unarmed reconnaissance aircraft, with cameras and side-looking airborne radar in nose. No search/fire control radar.
'Foxbat-C' (MiG-25U). Trainer, with two separate canopies in tandem. No radar.
'Foxbat-E' (MiG-25M). Single-seat interceptor, designed for high-speed 'straight and level' attack at high altitude. Large radar provides limited look-down/shoot-down capability comparable with 'Flogger'. Built primarily of arc-welded nickel steel, with titanium wing and tail leading-edges.
'Foxbat-F'. Basically similar to MiG-25M, but equipped to attack surface-to-air missile radars over long stand-off ranges. Armed with AS-11 ('Kilter') anti-radiation homing missiles. Dielectric panels on sides of nose, aft of radome. Entered service in 1988.

Data for 'Foxbat-E'

Engines: Two Tumansky R-15BD-300 turbojets, each rated at 24,700lb (110kN) thrust with afterburning.
Wing span: 45ft 9in (13.95m)
Length: 78ft 1¾in (23.82m)
Height: 20ft 0¼in (6.10m)
Maximum take-off weight: 82,500lb (37,425kg)
Maximum level speed: Mach 2.82 (1,860mph; 3,000km/h) at height; Mach 0.85 (645mph; 1,040km/h) at sea-level
Operational ceiling: 80,000ft (24,400m)
Combat radius: 700–900 miles (1,130–1,450km)

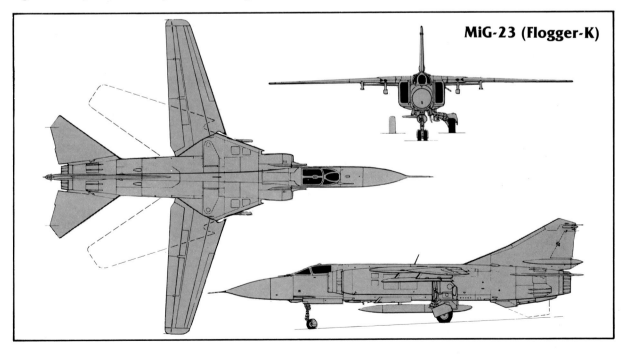

MiG-23 (Flogger-K)

MiG-25 (Foxbat-E)

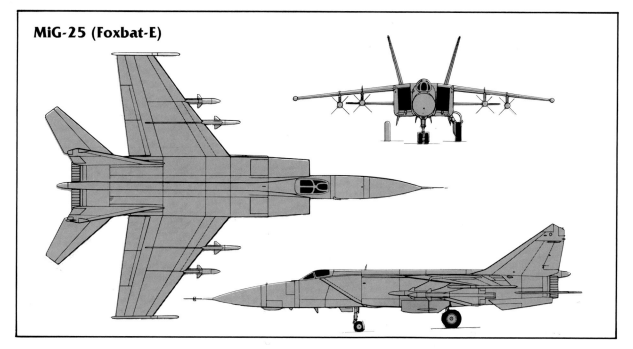

Operational Equipment and Armament:
  Radar ('Foxfire') in nose. Infra-red search/
  track sensor and radar warning system,
  ECCM and flare dispensers. Two infra-red
  and two semi-active radar homing AA-6
  ('Acrid') air-to-air missiles. Alternatively,
  two AA-7 ('Apex') and four AA-8 ('Aphid')
  or AA-11 ('Archer') air-to-air missiles.

MIKOYAN MiG-27

NATO Reporting Name: 'Flogger'
Ground-attack variant of MiG-23
First flight: not known
Estimated number operational in Soviet air
  forces: 825

Variants

'Flogger-D' (MiG-27). Basic airframe similar
  to that of MiG-23. Redesigned nose for
  operational equipment. Seat and canopy
  raised to improve pilot's view. Cockpit
  sides armoured. Low-pressure tyres.
  Gatling-type gun. Engine has fixed air
  intakes, instead of variable intakes, and
  two-position (on/off) afterburner nozzle to
  meet primary requirement of transonic
  speed at low altitude. Operational since
  second half of 1970s.
'Flogger-J' (MiG-27M). New nose, with lip
  at top and blister fairing below for sensor
  providing rearward designation capability
  for laser-guided bomb delivery. New IFF.
  External cockpit armour deleted.
  Wingroot leading-edge extensions
  added. Identified in 1981.

Data for 'Flogger-J'

Engine: Tumansky R-29B-300 turbojet,
  rated at 25,350lb (112.8kN) thrust with
  afterburning.
Wing span: 45ft 10in (13.965m) with wings
  spread; 25ft 6¼in (7.779m) with wings
  swept
Length: 56ft 1¼in (17.10m)
Height: 15ft 9¾in (4.82m)
Maximum take-off weight: 39,900–
  45,635lb (18,100–20,700kg)
Maximum level speed: Mach 1.77
  (1,165mph; 1,880km/h) at height; Mach
  1.10 (835mph; 1,345km/h) at sea-level

Operational ceiling: 45,900ft (14,000m)
Combat radius: 240 miles at low altitude,
  with 4,410lb (2,000kg) of bombs, two
  AA-2 ('Atoll') air-to-air missiles and ventral
  fuel tank
Operational Equipment and Armament:
  Laser rangefinder and laser target
  designator. Ranging radar. Radar warning
  system and flare dispensers. One 23mm
  six-barrel gun under fuselage. Up to
  9,920lb (4,500kg) of external stores,
  including tactical nuclear and conventional
  bombs, gun packs, and AS-7 ('Kerry'), AS-
  10 ('Karen'), AS-12 ('Kegler') and AS-14
  ('Kedge') air-to-surface missiles.

MIKOYAN MiG-29

NATO Reporting Name: 'Fulcrum'
Counter-air fighter with attack capability
First flight: late 1970s
Estimated number operational in Soviet air
  forces: more than 500

Variants

'Fulcrum-A' (MiG-29). Basic single-seat
  land-based fighter. Original ventral tail fins
  now deleted. Overwing dispensers for
  flares forward of dorsal fins. Look-down/
  shoot-down radar in nose. Hinged doors
  close air intakes during take-off and
  landing to prevent foreign object
  ingestion; engine airflow is then taken in
  through louvres in top of each wingroot
  extension.
'Fulcrum-B' (MiG-29UB). Combat trainer
  version of 'Fulcrum-A' with two crew in
  tandem under continuous canopy. Radar
  rangefinder replaces search radar.
  Underwing pylons retained.
'Fulcrum-C'. As 'Fulcrum-A', but with more
  deeply curved top to fuselage aft of
  canopy, containing extensive equipment.
'Fulcrum-D'. Carrier-based development of
  'Fulcrum-A', first seen in 1989. Folding
  outer wing panels, with ESM in bulged
  tips. Wingroot louvres and ducting
  deleted, permitting increased fuel
  tankage. Strengthened undercarriage,
  with arrester hook. In-flight refuelling

capability. Expected to serve on new
  aircraft-carrier *Tbilisi* and sister ships.

Data for 'Fulcrum-A'

Engines: Two Isotov RD-33 turbofans, each
  rated at 18,300lb (81.4kN) thrust with
  afterburning.
Wing span: 37ft 3¼in (11.36m)
Length including nose probe: 56ft 10in
  (17.32m)
Height: 15ft 6¼in (4.73m)
Maximum take-off weight: 39,700lb
  (18,000kg)
Maximum level speed: Mach 2.3
  (1,520mph; 2,440km/h) at height; Mach
  1.06 (805mph; 1,300km/h) at sea-level
Operational ceiling: 56,000ft (17,000m)
Maximum range: 1,300 miles (2,100km)
Operational Equipment and Armament:
  Search-while-scan pulse Doppler radar.
  Infra-red search/track sensor and laser
  rangefinder slaved to pilot's helmet-
  mounted target designator. Radar
  warning system, ECM and flare
  dispensers. One 30mm gun in port
  wingroot. Typical armament of six
  medium-range radar homing AA-10
  ('Alamo-A') and/or close-range infra-red
  homing AA-11 ('Archer') air-to-air
  missiles. Provision for carrying AA-9
  ('Amos') and AA-8 ('Aphid') missiles. For
  ground attack, bombs and rockets can be
  carried.

Pictures notes

28. Formation of MiG-29s taking off; Tu-
  160 and Il-78 on the ground.
45. Pilot in cockpit of MiG-29.
47. Loading an air-to-air missile on MiG-
  29.
48. MiG-29 inverted at top of a loop.
49. 'Aphid' air-to-air missiles being fired
  from MiG-29s.
50. Pilots of MiG-29 formation team.

SUKHOI Su-17

NATO Reporting Name: 'Fitter'
Variable-geometry tactical attack aircraft
First flight: 1967

MiG-27 (Flogger-J)

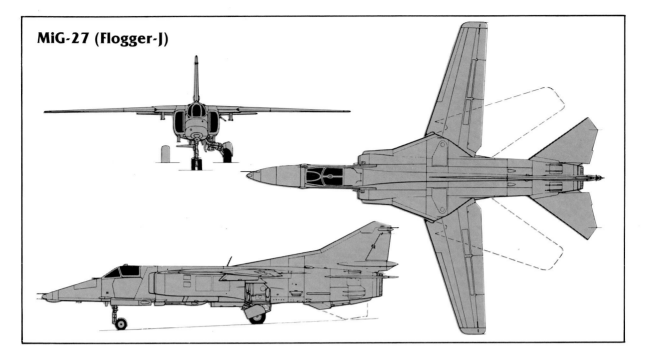

MiG-29 (Fulcrum-A)

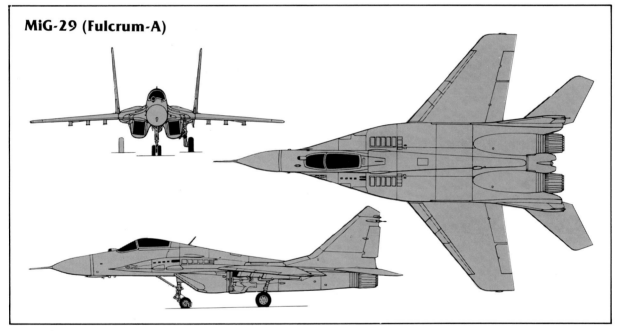

Estimated number operational in Soviet air forces: 1,125

Variants

'Fitter-C' (Su-17). Basic single-seat attack aircraft. First operational in 1971. Sweepback of wings variable manually at 28°, 45° and 62°.

'Fitter-D' (Su-17M). As basic Su-17, but forward fuselage lengthened by 15in (38cm) and drooped 3° to improve view from cockpit. Undernose pod for Doppler navigation radar. Laser rangefinder in intake centre-body.

'Fitter-E' (Su-17U). Tandem two-seat trainer version of Su-17M, without undernose pod. Additional fuel in deepened dorsal spine fairing. One gun deleted, from port wingroot.

'Fitter-G' (Su-17UM). Combat-capable two-

seat version of Su-17M-3. Taller tail fin and shallow, removable, ventral fin. Laser rangefinder in centre-body. Starboard wingroot gun only.

'Fitter-H' (Su-17M-1/3). The Su-17M-1 is an improved single-seater, with the same deepened spine and tail modifications as the Su-17UM. Its nose is deepened to enclose the Doppler radar carried previously in an undernose pod. Gun in each wingroot. About 165 'Fitter-H/Ks' are used for tactical reconnaissance, typically with a centre-line sensor pod, an active ECM pod under the port wingroot and two underwing fuel tanks. The Su-17M-3 introduced improved avionics in the early 1980s, plus a launcher for an air-to-air self-defence missile between each pair of underwing pylons.

'Fitter-K' (Su-17M-4). Further improved single-seater, identified by small cooling

air intake at front of dorsal fin.

Data for 'Fitter-K' (Except dimensions where indicated)

Engine: Lyulka AL-21F-3 turbojet, rated at 24,700lb (110kN) thrust with afterburning.

Wing span: 45ft 3in (13.80m) with wings spread; 32ft 10in (10.00m) with wings swept

Length ('Fitter-C') including nose probes: 61ft 6¼in (18.75m)

Height ('Fitter-C'): 16ft 5in (5.00m)

Maximum take-off weight: 42,990lb (19,500kg)

Maximum level speed: Mach 2.09 (1,380mph; 2,220km/h) at height; Mach 1.14 (870mph; 1,400km/h) at sea-level

Operational ceiling: 49,865ft (15,200m)

Maximum range: 1,430 miles (2,300km) at height; 870 miles (1,400km) at sea-level

179

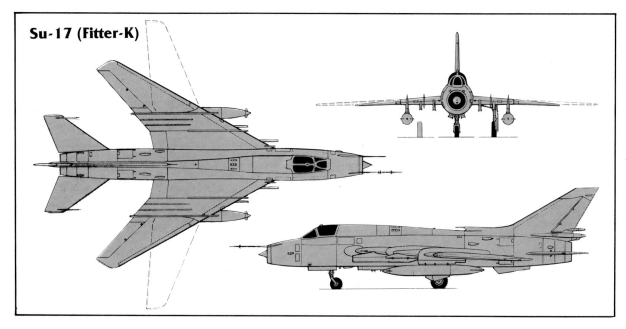

Su-17 (Fitter-K)

Operational Equipment and Armament: I band ranging radar ('High Fix'). Radar warning system. Flare dispensers in four containers on each side of spine fairing. Two 30mm guns in wingroots. Up to 9,370lb (4,250kg) of external stores, including two self-defence AA-2 ('Atoll'), AA-8 ('Aphid') or AA-11 ('Archer') infrared missiles, nuclear weapons, rocket pods, air-to-surface rockets, 23mm gun pods, AS-7 ('Kerry'), AS-9 ('Kyle') and AS-10 ('Karen') air-to-surface missiles, bombs or a tactical reconnaissance pod.

Picture notes
51. Pilot of Su-17M-4 preparing for flight.
54. Pilot in cockpit of Su-17, with two-seat Su-17UM ('Fitter-G') in background.
59. Night take-off by Su-17, using full afterburning.
63. Su-17M-4 firing an air-to-surface rocket.

SUKHOI Su-24
NATO Reporting Name: 'Fencer'
Variable-geometry tactical and strategic attack aircraft. Two crew side by side.
First flight: 1969–70
Estimated number operational in Soviet air forces: 800

Variants
'Fencer-A'. Early production version, identified by rectangular rear fuselage surrounding jet nozzles. Known initially as Su-19.
'Fencer-B'. Basically as 'Fencer-A', but with deeply dished bottom skin between jet nozzles at tail. Larger brake-parachute container under rudder.
'Fencer-C'. Introduced in 1981, with major equipment changes. Identified by multiple probe, instead of single probe, on nose. Triangular radar warning receiver fairings on side of each intake duct and on each side of fin tip. Fin leading-edge extended forward slightly except for tip.
'Fencer-D' (Su-24MK). First version equipped to refuel in flight, introduced in 1983. Sometimes with large wing fences, integral with extended wingroot pylon on each side for AS-14 ('Kedge') missile.

Electro-optical sensor pod behind nosewheel bay. Single long nose probe.
'Fencer-E'. Maritime reconnaissance version of 'Fencer-D', retaining ability to carry air-to-surface missiles. Used by tactical air force and naval air units.
'Fencer-?'. Electronic jamming, signals intelligence (SIGINT) and reconnaissance version, to replace veteran Yak-28 ('Brewer-E').

Data for 'Fencer-D'
Engines: Two Lyulka AL-21F-3A turbojets, each rated at 24,700lb (110kN) thrust with afterburning.
Wing span: 57ft 10in (17.63m) with wings spread; 34ft 0in (10.36m) with wings swept
Length: 80ft 5¾in (24.53m)
Height: 16ft 3¾in (4.97m)
Maximum take-off weight: 87,520lb (39,700kg)
Maximum level speed: Mach 2.18 (1,440mph; 2,315km/h) at height; Mach 1.15 (875mph; 1,405km/h) at sea-level
Operational ceiling: 57,400ft (17,500m)
Combat radius: 200–650 miles (322–1,050km) without in-flight refuelling, depending on cruising height
Operational Equipment and Armament: Radar in nose. Specially developed long-range navigation system and electro-optical weapons systems permit day/night and poor weather penetration of hostile airspace to deliver bombs and missiles within 180ft (55m) of target. Eight pylons under fuselage and wings for 17,635lb (8,000kg) of nuclear weapons, air-to-surface guided missiles such as AS-7 ('Kerry'), AS-10 ('Karen'), AS-11 ('Kilter'), AS-12 ('Kegler'), AS-13 ('Kingbolt') and AS-14 ('Kedge'), 57 to 370mm rockets, up to 36 bombs, 23mm gun pods, and external fuel tanks. Six-barrel 30mm Gatling-type gun under fuselage.

SUKHOI Su-25
NATO Reporting Name: 'Frogfoot'
Close support aircraft
First flight: 22 February 1975
Estimated number operational in Soviet air forces: 300

Variants
'Frogfoot-A' (Su-25K). Single-seat close support aircraft. Laser guidance system is claimed to place weapons within 16ft (5m) of a target over a stand-off range of 12.5 miles (20km). All-welded cockpit is made of titanium armour. Engines will run on kerosene, motor gasoline or diesel oil.
'Frogfoot-B' (Su-25UB). Tandem two-seat trainer, with raised rear seat and canopy. Taller tain fin. All weapons retained. Has been fitted with arrester hook for naval use.
Frogfoot-B' (Su-25UT). As Su-25UB, but for advanced flying training only, without weapons.

Data for 'Frogfoot-A'
Engines: Two Tumansky R-195 turbojets, each rated at 9,921lb (44.18kN) thrust
Wing span: 47ft 1½in (14.36m)
Length: 50ft 11½in (15.53m)
Height: 15ft 9in (4.80m)
Maximum take-off weight: 32,187–38,800lb (14,600–17,600kg)
Maximum level speed: Mach 0.8 (606mph; 975km/h) at sea-level
Operational ceiling: 22,965ft (7,000m)
Maximum range: 466 miles (750km) at sea-level; 776 miles (1,250km) at height
Operational Equipment and Armament: Laser rangefinder and target designator in nose. Radar warning system, IFF and chaff/flare dispensers. One 30mm twin-barrel gun in front fuselage. Two AA-2 ('Atoll') or AA-8 ('Aphid') self-defence air-to-air missiles. Up to 9,700lb (4,400kg) of external stores, including 23mm gun pods, rockets, laser-guided missiles and high-explosive, incendiary, anti-personnel and chemical cluster bombs. Weapons load to be increased to 14,100lb (6,400kg).

Picture notes
68. Su-25K landing, with wingtip airbrakes open.

SUKHOI Su-27
NATO Reporting Name: 'Flanker'
Primary air-to-air combat and escort fighter of the Soviet air forces
First flight: 20 May 1977

Su-24 (Fencer-D)

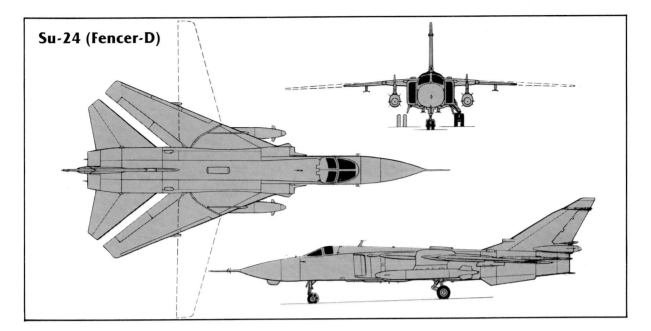

Su-25 (Frogfoot-A)

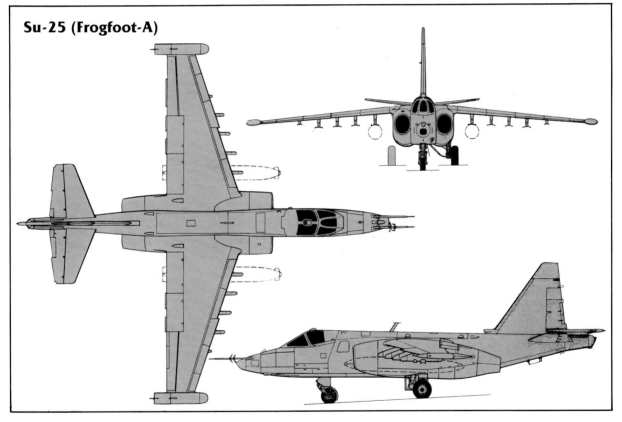

Estimated number operational in Soviet air forces: 200

Variants

'Flanker-B' (Su-27). Single-seat fighter, extensively redesigned compared with prototypes; first flown on 20 April 1981.

'Flanker-B' variant 2. As 'Flanker-B' but with moveable foreplanes.

'Flanker-C' (Su-27UB). Combat-capable tandem two-seat training version of 'Flanker-B'.

'Flanker-D' Naval version for operation from aircraft-carriers, with added movable foreplanes. Folding outer wings, long tailcone deleted, twin nosewheels, added arrester hook and flight-refuelling capability. Provision for 'buddy' flight-refuelling pack on centre-line pylon between engine ducts. Evaluated on Soviet Navy carrier *Tbilisi* in 1989–90.

'Flanker-?'. Side-by-side two-seat version of 'Flanker-D' for training. No radar or underwing pylons.

Data for 'Flanker-B'

Engines: Two Lyulka AL-31F turbofans, each rated at 27,557lb (123.85kN) thrust with afterburning.

Wing span: 48ft 2¾in (14.70m)

Length excluding nose probe: 71ft 11½in (21.935m)

Height: 19ft 5½in (5.932m)

Maximum take-off weight: 48,500–66,135lb (22,000–30,000kg)

Maximum level speed: Mach 2.35 (1,550mph; 2,500km/h) at height; Mach 1.1 (835mph; 1,345km/h) at sea-level

Operational ceiling: 59,055ft (18,000m)

Maximum range: 2,485 miles (4,000km)

Operational Equipment and Armament: Track-while-scan pulse Doppler radar with look-down/shoot-down capability. Infra-red search/track sensor and laser rangefinder slaved to pilot's helmet-

Su-27 (Flanker-B)

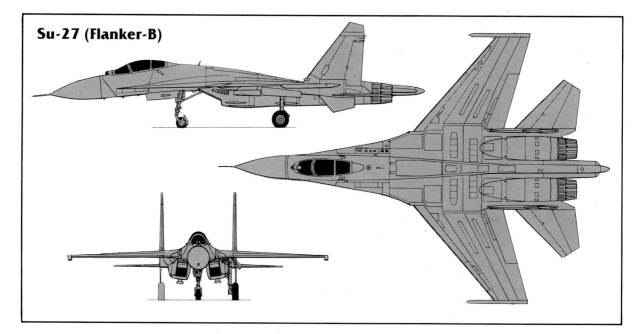

mounted target designator. Radar warning system and chaff/flare dispensers. One 30mm gun in starboard wingroot. Typical air-to-air missile armament of two short-range semi-active radar homing AA-10A ('Alamo-A'), two short-range infrared homing AA-10B ('Alamo-B'), two long-range semi-active radar homing AA-10C ('Alamo-C'), and four AA-11 ('Archer') or AA-8 ('Aphid') close-range infra-red missiles. AA-9 ('Amos') missiles can be carried instead of AA-10s.

Picture notes
81. Su-27 landing, with airbrake open above fuselage.
82. The Soviet Navy aircraft carrier *Tbilisi*.
83. Su-27 (Flanker-D) on the *Tbilisi*.
84—86. Spreading the wings of the naval Su-27 (Flanker-D).
87. Su-27 taking off on the *Tbsilisi*.

88. Su-27 leaving the *Tbilisi*'s ski-jump ramp.
89. Su-27 landing on the *Tbilisi*.
90. Still hooked to an arrester wire, the Su-27 nears the end of *Tbilisi*'s angled deck.

YAKOVLEV Yak-38
NATO Reporting Name: 'Forger'
Ship-based V/STOL combat aircraft, carried on Soviet Navy carriers.
First flight: 1971
Estimated number operational in Soviet Navy: 70

Variants
'Forger-A'. Single-seat combat aircraft, with primary roles of attack on small ships, fleet defence against shadowing maritime patrol aircraft and reconnaissance. Short take-off achieved by automatic control

system that switches lift engines to full power and rotates to a 10° forward-facing position the exhaust nozzles of the main turbojet at the optimum point in the take-off run. First seen at sea in 1976.
'Forger-B'. Tandem two-seat trainer with lengthened fuselage and drooped nose to provide improved view for crew. No ranging radar or weapons.

Data for 'Forger-A'
Engines: One Tumansky R-27V-300 turbojet, rated at 15,300lb (68kN) thrust, exhausting through a single pair of vectoring side nozzles aft of wings. Two tandem Koliesov/Rybinsk RD-36-35FVR liftjets, each rated at 6,725lb thrust (30kN), mounted at 13° rearward-inclined angle immediately behind cockpit.
Wing span: 24ft 0in (7.32m)

Yak-38 (Forger-A)

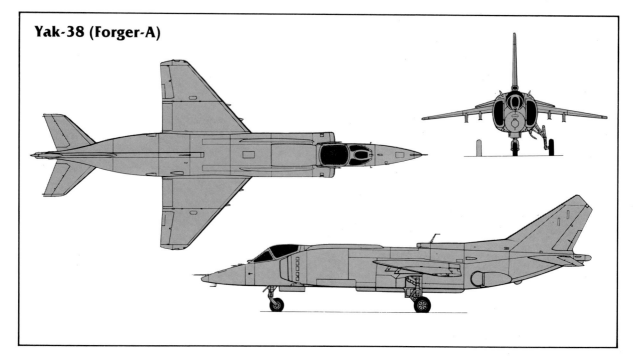

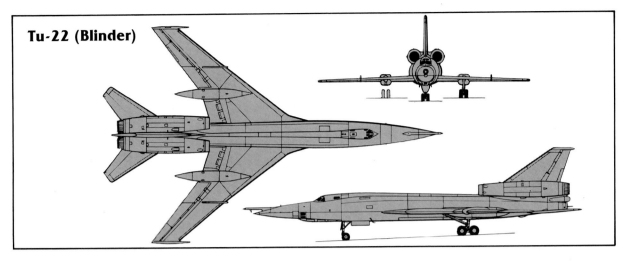

Tu-22 (Blinder)

Width, wings folded: 16ft 0in (4.88m)
Length: 50ft 10¼in (15.50m)
Height: 14ft 4in (4.37m)
Maximum take-off weight: 25,795lb
(11,700kg)
Maximum level speed: Mach 0.95
(627mph; 1,009km/h) at height; Mach 0.8
(608mph; 978km/h) at sea-level
Operational ceiling: 39,375ft (12,000m)
Combat radius: 150–230 miles (240–
370km) with maximum weapons,
depending on cruising height
Operational Equipment and Armament:
Ranging radar and IFF. Automatic control
and stability system for take-off and
landing. Four underwing pylons for up to
7,935lb (3,600kg) of 23mm twin-barrel
gun pods, rocket packs, bombs of up to
1,100lb (500kg) each, AS-7 ('Kerry') air-
to-surface missiles, armour-piercing anti-
ship missiles, AA-8 ('Aphid') close-range
infra-red air-to-air missiles, and external
fuel tanks.

Picture notes

91. The aircraft on the right of this
photograph is a two-seat 'Forger-B'.

TUPOLEV Tu-22

NATO Reporting Name: 'Blinder'
Supersonic bomber and maritime patrol
aircraft
First flight: about 1961
Estimated number operational in Soviet air
forces: 125

Variants

'Blinder-A'. Original reconnaissance
bomber, carrying nuclear and
conventional bombs in fuselage weapons
bay. First Soviet bomber capable of
supersonic flight for short periods.
Engines mounted above fuselage on each
side of fin. Crew of three in tandem seats.
'Blinder-B'. Basically as 'Blinder-A', but able
to carry AS-4 ('Kitchen') missile recessed
in weapons bay. Larger nose radar. Partially
retractable flight-refuelling probe above nose.
'Blinder-C'. Maritime reconnaissance
version, with camera windows in weapons
bay doors. Some aircraft equipped for
ECM and electronic intelligence roles.
Flight-refuelling probe standard.
'Blinder-D'. Training version, with stepped-
up cockpit for instructor aft of standard
flight deck.

Data for 'Blinder-B'

Engines: Two Koliesov VD-7 turbojets, each
rated at 30,900lb (137.5kN) thrust with
afterburning.
Wing span: 78ft 0in (23.75m)
Length: 132ft 11½in (40.53m)
Height: 35ft 0in (10.67m)
Maximum take-off weight: 185,000lb
(83,900kg)
Maximum level speed: Mach 1.4 (920mph;
1,480km/h) at height
Maximum combat radius: 1,490 miles
(2,400km)
Operational Equipment and Armament:
Radar in nose. Chaff/flare dispensers. One
23mm gun in radar-directed tail turret.
AS-4 ('Kitchen') missile carries nuclear or
conventional warhead up to 285 miles
(460km) at Mach 4.6 (approx. 3,000mph/
4,850km/h at altitude). Conventional free-
fall bombs optional.

TUPOLEV Tu-22M

NATO Reporting Name: 'Backfire'
Variable-geometry supersonic bomber and
maritime patrol aircraft
First flight: 1971

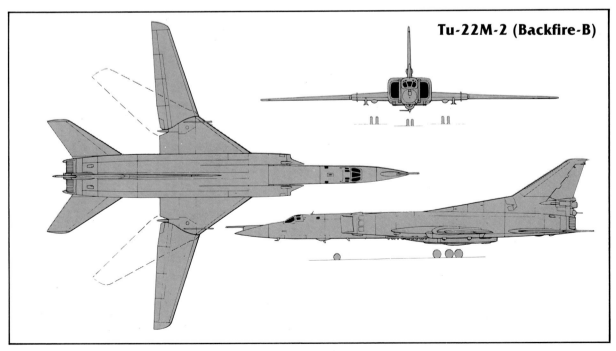

Tu-22M-2 (Backfire-B)

Estimated number operational in Soviet air forces: more than 350

Variants
'Backfire-B' (Tu-22M-2). Initial series production version, often referred to in West as Tu-26. Wing sweep variable from 20° to 65°. Slightly inclined lateral air intakes. Fairing above nose usually replaces optional flight-refuelling probe. Armed normally with one or two AS-4 ('Kitchen') air-to-surface missiles. Optional racks for 1,100lb (500kg) bombs under air intake trunks. Crew of four.

'Backfire-C' (Tu-22M-3). Differs from Tu-22M-2 in having wedge-type air intakes, upturned nosecone and no visible flight-refuelling probe. Single gun in tail turret.

Data for 'Backfire-B'
Engines: Two unidentified turbofans, each with probable rating of more than 45,000lb (200kN) thrust with afterburning.
Wing span: 112ft 6½in (34.30m) with wings spread; 76ft 9¼in (23.40m) with wings swept
Length: 129ft 11in (39.60m)
Height: 35ft 5¼in (10.80m)
Maximum take-off weight: 286,600lb (130,000kg)
Maximum level speed: Mach 2.0 (1,320mph; 2,125km/h) at height; Mach 0.9 (685mph; 1,100km/h) at sea-level
Maximum combat radius: 2,485 miles (4,000km)
Operational Equipment and Armament: Bombing and navigation radar ('Down Beat') in nose. Window for video camera under front fuselage to assist weapon aiming. Two 23mm twin-barrel guns in radar-directed tail mounting. One AS-4 ('Kitchen') air-to-surface missile recessed under fuselage, or one under each fixed inboard wing panel, or 26,450lb (12,000kg) of bombs. Provision for racks for twelve 1,100lb (500kg) bombs under intake trunks.

TUPOLEV Tu-95 and Tu-142
NATO Reporting Name: 'Bear'
Long-range bomber, maritime reconnaissance, anti-submarine and command communications aircraft
First flight: 1954
Estimated number operational in Soviet air forces: 240

Variants
'Bear-D'. Maritime reconnaissance Tu-95 with glazed nose, undernose radar ('Short Horn'), large underbelly I band surface search radar ('Big Bulge'), electronic intelligence (ELINT) fairings and nose refuelling probe. No attack weapons. Tasks include pinpointing distant targets for missile launch crews on ships and aircraft. Armed with six 23mm guns in three turrets.

'Bear-E'. Reconnaissance version of Tu-95 with cameras in weapons bay, ELINT fairings and refuelling probe. Armament as 'Bear-D'.

'Bear-F'. First Tu-142, with new wings, longer front fuselage for relief crew and improved galley, smaller J band underbelly radar than 'Bear-D' mounted farther forward, no ELINT fairings, and only two guns in tail turret. Two bays for sonobuoys, torpedoes and depth-charges in rear fuselage. Usually with magnetic anomaly detection (MAD) boom on fin tip.

'Bear-G'. Bomber and ELINT version of Tu-95, armed with two AS-4 ('Kitchen') air-to-surface missiles. New undernose radar ('Down Beat'), ECM 'thimble' under nose refuelling probe and four small ECM pods under fuselage. 'Solid' tailcone containing special equipment. Only two 23mm guns, in ventral turret.

'Bear-H'. Tu-142 airframe, but shortened to length of Tu-95. Six AS-15 ('Kent') air-launched cruise missiles carried on

internal rotary launcher, with provision for two more under each wingroot. Larger and deeper nose radome. Small fin tip fairing. No ELINT blisters. One or two 23mm twin-barrel guns in tail turret. More than 70 built to date. Operational since 1984.

'Bear J'. Able to trail several kilometres of wire antenna from pod under fuselage, to maintain VLF communications between national command authorities and nuclear missile submarines at sea. Airframe similar to 'Bear-F'. Many added antennas and fairings.

Data for 'Bear-F'
Engines: Four Kuznetsov NK-12MV turboprops, each rated at 14,795ehp (11,033kW)
Wing span: 167ft 8in (51.10m)
Length: 162ft 5in (49.50m)
Height: 39ft 9in (12.12m)
Maximum take-off weight: 414,470lb (188,000kg)
Maximum level speed: 575mph (925km/h) at 25,000ft (7,620m)
Operational ceiling: about 41,000ft (12,500m)
Maximum combat radius: 5,150 miles (8,285km)
Operational Equipment and Armament: As described under individual variants, plus chaff/flare dispensers.

TUPOLEV Tu-160
NATO Reporting Name: 'Blackjack'
Long-range supersonic strategic bomber, with variable-geometry wings
First flight: unknown
Estimated number operational in Soviet air forces: 24

Variants
'Blackjack-A' (Tu-160). Only known version,

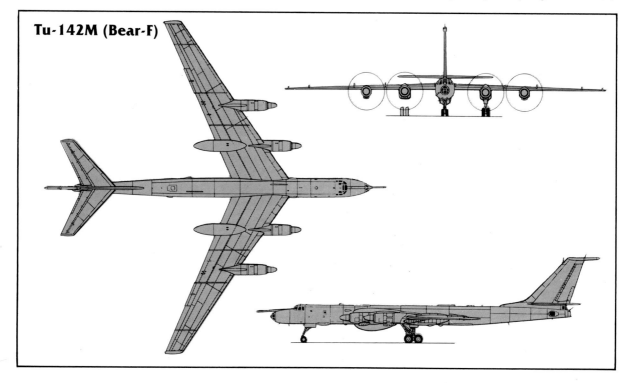

Tu-142M (Bear-F)

Tu-160 (Blackjack)

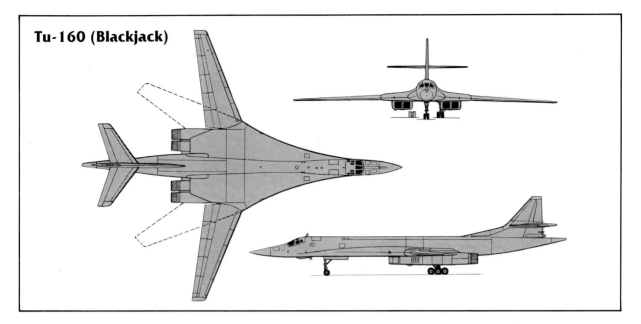

designed as primary strategic attack aircraft of Soviet Union. About 20 per cent longer than its US counterpart, the B-1B, with much higher supersonic speed and greater unrefuelled combat radius. Flight-refuelling capability assumed. Current AS-15 air-launched cruise missiles (ALCMs) are expected to be replaced soon by supersonic AS-19s with a range of 2,000 miles (3,200km). Can be used for subsonic cruise/supersonic dash at up to 60,000ft (18,300m) or transonic penetration at low altitude. Entered service in 1988. Production of about 100 expected.

Data for 'Blackjack-A' (estimated)
Engines: Four 55,115lb (245kN) thrust afterburning turbofans identified to date only as 'Type R'.

Wing span: 182ft 9in (55.70m) with wings spread; 110ft 0in (33.75m) with wings swept
Length: 177ft 0in (54.00m)
Height: 42ft 0in (12.80m)
Maximum take-off weight: 606,260lb (275,000kg)
Maximum level speed: Mach 1.88 (1,240mph; 2,000km/h) at height
Maximum combat radius: 4,535 miles (7,300km)
Operational Equipment and Armament: Nose radar provides terrain-following capability. Fairing under front fuselage for video camera to facilitate weapon aiming. Normal offensive weapons, carried on two rotary launchers, are 24 AS-16 ('Kickback') short-range attack missiles or 12 AS-15 ('Kent') subsonic ALCMs with a range of 1,850 miles (3,000km) carrying

a 200kT nuclear warhead. Up to 36,000lb (16,330kg) of nuclear or conventional bombs can be carried instead of missiles. There are no guns.

Picture notes
115. The fin of the Tu-160 is a one-piece all-moving surface, as this photograph shows.

TUPOLEV Tu-16
NATO Reporting Name: 'Badger'
Medium-range bomber, maritime reconnaissance/attack and flight-refuelling tanker aircraft
First flight: Winter of 1951/52
Estimated number operational in Soviet air forces: 625

Variants
'Badger-A' (Tu-16A). Basic strategic

Tu-16 (Badger-F)

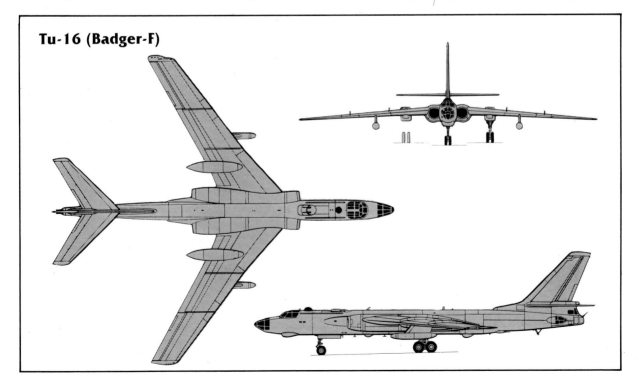

bomber, carrying up to 19,800lb (9,000kg) of nuclear or conventional free-fall bombs. Glazed nose with undernose radome. Defensive armament of seven 23mm guns. About 20 aircraft converted into flight-refuelling tankers for air forces and 70 for the Soviet naval air force. These utilize a unique wingtip-to-wingtip technique to refuel other Tu-16s, or a probe-and-drogue system to refuel Tu-22s.

'Badger-C' (Tu-16K-10). Anti-ship version carrying AS-2 ('Kipper') missile recessed in fuselage. No provision for free-fall bombs. Wide nose radome ('Puff Ball') instead of glazing and nose gun. 'Badger-C Mod' carries one or two underwing AS-6 ('Kingfish') missiles.

'Badger-D' (Tu-16R). Maritime/electronic reconnaissance aircraft. Similar to 'Badger-C' but with larger undernose radome and three smaller radomes under weapons bay.

'Badger-E'. Photographic and electronic reconnaissance aircraft. As 'Badger-A' but with cameras in weapons bay and two radomes under fuselage.

'Badger-F' (Tu-16R). As 'Badger-E' but with ELINT pod under each wing.

'Badger-G'. As 'Badger-A' but with two AS-5 ('Kelt') missiles underwing. Free-fall bombing capability retained. 'Badger-G Mod' carries one or two AS-6 ('Kingfish') missiles, able to carry a nuclear warhead 250 miles (400km) at Mach 3. Large radome under centre fuselage, instead of chin radome.

'Badger-H' (Tu-16PP). Chaff-dispensing ECM aircraft to protect strike force. Dispensers in weapons bay, with small radomes fore and aft. Glazed nose and chin radome.

'Badger-J' (Tu-16PP). ECM jamming/ELINT aircraft. Canoe-shape radome under weapons bay and flat-plate antennas at wingtips. Glazed nose.

'Badger-K' (Tu-16R). Electronic reconnaissance variant with glazed nose and six underfuselage radomes and blister fairings.

Data for 'Badger-G'
Engines: Two Mikulin RD-3M-500 turbojets, each rated at 20,920lb (93.05kN) thrust.
Wing span: 108ft 3in (32.99m)
Length: 114ft 2in (34.80m)
Height: 34ft 0in (10.36m)
Normal take-off weight: 165,350lb (75,000kg)
Maximum level speed: 616mph (992km/h) at 19,700ft (6,000m)
Operational ceiling: 40,350ft (12,300m)
Combat radius: 1,955 miles (3,150km)
Operational Equipment and Armament: Undernose bombing and navigation radar. Radar warning system. Seven 23mm guns, in pairs in three turrets and singly in nose. Attack weapons as described in model listing.

Picture notes
117. This photograph shows the unique wingtip-to-wingtip flight refuelling technique used by the Tu-16.

MYASISHCHEV M-3
NATO Reporting Name: 'Bison'
Flight-refuelling tanker aircraft
First flight ('Bison-A' bomber): 1953
Estimated number operational in Soviet air forces: 40

Variants
The only version of 'Bison' still operational is the flight-refuelling tanker conversion of now-retired strategic bombers.

Data for 'Bison-A'
Engines: Four Mikulin AM-3D turbojets, each rated at 19,180lb (85.3kN) thrust.
Wing span: 165ft 7½in (50.48m)
Length: 154ft 10in (47.20m)

Maximum take-off weight: 350,000lb (158,750kg)
Maximum level speed: 620mph (998km/h) at height
Operational ceiling: 45,000ft (13,700m)
Maximum combat radius: 3,480 miles (5,600km) as bomber
Operational Equipment and Armament: Tanker version of 'Bison' is equipped with a hose reel to refuel in flight single examples of the 'Backfire', 'Bear' and 'Blinder' bombers, using the probe-and-drogue technique.

ILYUSHIN Il-78
NATO Reporting Name: 'Midas'
Flight-refuelling tanker aircraft
First flight: unknown
Estimated number in service in Soviet air forces: 12

Variants
The only version identified to date is an adaptation of the standard Il-76MD transport aircraft, with generally similar characteristics. It is equipped as a three-point tanker, with refuelling pods of the same type under the outer wings and on the port side of the rear fuselage. The rear turret is unarmed and serves as an observation station during refuelling missions. 'Midas' entered service in 1987, in support of Soviet strategic and tactical aircraft.

ANTONOV An-124
NATO Reporting Name: 'Condor'
Long-range heavy freight transport
First flight: 26 December 1982
Estimated number available to Soviet air forces: 20

Variants
Only the basic transport has been identified to date. Largest production military transport in the world, it can carry the

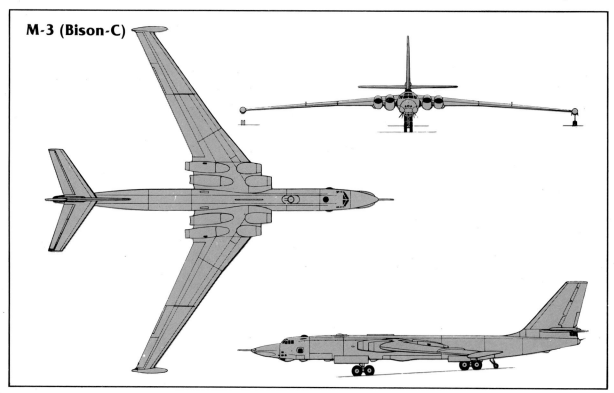

M-3 (Bison-C)

Il-78 (Midas)

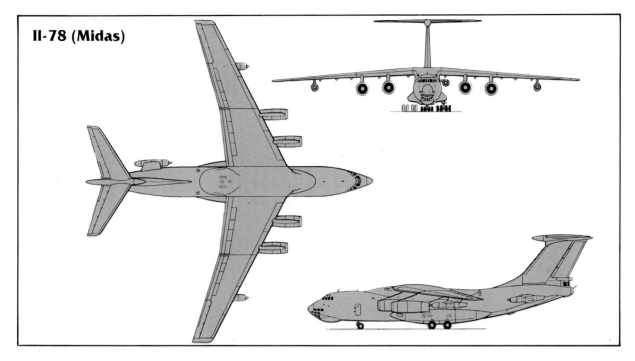

largest Soviet main battle tanks, guided missile systems and other heavy or bulky loads. The main cabin is loaded and unloaded via an upward-hinged nose and rear ramp doorway. Overhead gantries and winches in the main cabin assist freight handling. The main undercarriage legs can be deflated, so that the aircraft 'kneels' during front loading. The 24-wheel undercarriage permits operation from unprepared fields, hard packed snow and ice-covered swamplands. A rear upper deck contains seats for 88 passengers. The main freight hold is too lightly pressurized for passenger carrying,

except at low altitude in an emergency.

Data
Engines: Four Lotarev D-18T turbofans, each rated at 51,590lb (229.5kN) thrust
Wing span: 240ft 5¾in (73.30m)
Length: 226ft 8½in (69.10m)
Height: 68ft 2¼in (20.78m)
Maximum take-off weight: 892,872lb (405,000kg)
Maximum cruising speed: 537mph (865km/h) at 32,800–39,370ft (10,000–12,000m)
Range: 2,795 miles (4,500km) with maximum payload; 10,250 miles

(16,500km) with maximum fuel
Operational Equipment and Armament: Weather radar and ground mapping/navigation radar in nose and undernose. Satellite navigation system. No armament. Maximum payload 330,693lb (150,000kg).

ANTONOV An-22
NATO Reporting Name: 'Cock'
Long-range heavy turboprop transport
First flight: 27 February 1965
Estimated number available to Soviet air forces: 45

An-124 (Condor)

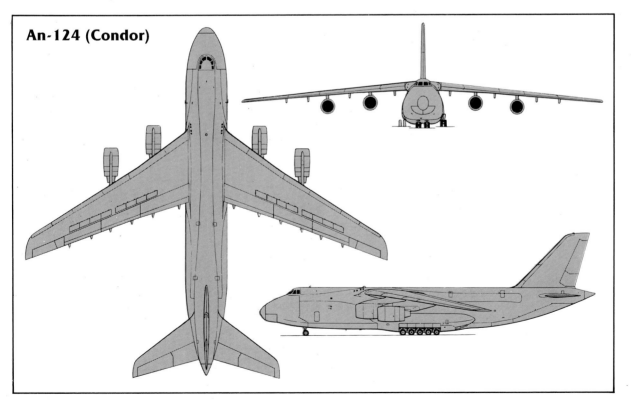

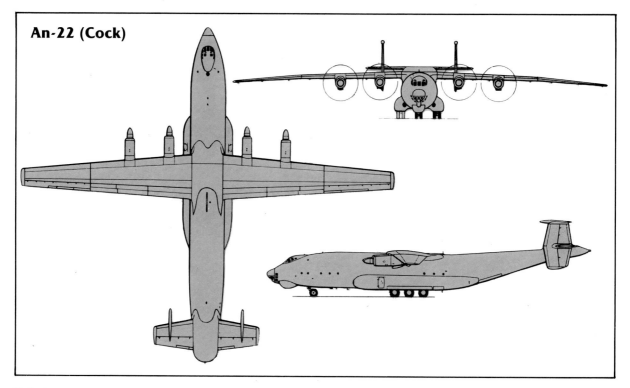

An-22 (Cock)

Variants
Only one version known. About 75 built, to
carry tanks and heavy equipment of
Soviet armed forces, and large civilian
loads. Crew of five or six. Cabin for 28–29
persons, such as crews of vehicles, missile
launch personnel and others associated
with freight carried in main cabin. Rear
loading doors and ramp, travelling
gantries on rails in top of hold, and
winches for quick and easy handling of
heavy or bulky loads.

Data
Engines: Four Kuznetsov NK-12MA
turboprops, each rated at 15,000shp
(11,185kW).
Wing span: 211ft 4in (64.40m)
Length: 190ft 0in (57.92m)
Height: 41ft 1½in (12.53m)
Maximum take-off weight: 551,160lb
(250,000kg)
Maximum level speed: 460mph (740km/h)
Range: 3,100 miles (5,000km) with
maximum payload; 6,800 miles
(10,950km) with maximum fuel
Operational Equipment and Armament:
Weather and navigation radar in nose and
undernose radomes. No armament.
Maximum payload 176,350lb (80,000kg).

ANTONOV An-12
NATO Reporting Name: 'Cub'
Medium-range transport, electronic
intelligence and ECM aircraft
First flight: 1958
Estimated number operational in Soviet air
forces: 350

Variants
'Cub'. Basic paratroop and freight transport,
in service since 1959, as An-12BP. Crew
of six, 90 troops or 60 paratroops, or
freight. Rear loading door, but no integral
loading ramp. Rear gun turret standard.
'Cub-A'. Electronic intelligence (ELINT)
aircraft. Blade aerials above fuselage,

behind flight deck, and other changes.
'Cub-B'. ELINT version with two small
radomes under centre fuselage, and other
changes.
'Cub-C'. ECM version with several tons of
equipment in cabin, palletized jammers in
belly, and chaff/flare dispensers. Special
electronics in 'solid' tailcone replace tail
turret.
'Cub-D'. Another ECM variant, with
equipment different from that of 'Cub-C'.

Data for standard An-12BP transport
Engines: Four Ivchenko AI-20K turboprops,
each rated at 3,945ehp (2,942kW).
Wing span: 124ft 8in (38.00m)
Length: 108ft 7¼in (33.10m)
Height: 34ft 6½in (10.53m)
Maximum take-off weight: 134,480lb
(61,000kg)
Maximum level speed: 482mph (777km/h)
Operational ceiling: 33,500ft (10,200m)
Range: 2,236 miles (3,600km) with
maximum payload; 3,540 miles
(5,700km) with maximum fuel
Operational Equipment and Armament:
Navigation and weather radar under nose.
Two 23mm guns in manned rear turret.
Maximum payload 44,090lb (20,000kg).

ILYUSHIN Il-76
NATO Reporting Name: 'Candid'
Medium/long-range transport
First flight: 25 March 1971
Estimated number available to Soviet air
forces: 450, plus 125 Aeroflot 'Candid-As'
without rear turret.

Variants
'Candid-B' (Il-76M). Basic version, differing
from civil 'Candid-A' in having a rear gun
turret. Crew of seven, including freight
handlers. Main hold is loaded and
unloaded via rear ramp door. Overhead
travelling cranes and winches facilitate
loading and positioning of cargo. Loads
can include vehicles, missile systems,
containers and pallets, with folding seats

along sidewalls for accompanying
personnel. Entire interior can be
pressurized, to permit carriage of 140
troops or 125 paratroops on palletized
seat modules. Replacement of air force
An-12BPs has been under way since
1974.
'Candid-B' (Il-76MD). Improved version
with D-30KP-1 engines that maintain their
full rating at high temperatures. Maximum
take-off weight increased to 418,875lb
(190,000kg), payload to 105,820lb
(48,000kg), and range extended by 745
miles (1,200km) by increased fuel
capacity. Entered service in early 1980s.

Data for Il-76M
Engines: Four Soloviev D-30KP turbofans,
each rated at 26,455lb (117.7kN) thrust.
Wing span: 165ft 8in (50.50m)
Length: 152ft 10¼in (46.59m)
Height: 48ft 5in (14.76m)
Maximum take-off weight: 374,785lb
(170,000kg)
Maximum level speed: 528mph (850km/h)
at 29,500–39,370ft (9,000–12,000m)
Range: 3,100 miles (5,000km) with
88,185lb (40,000kg) payload; 4,163
miles (6,700km) with maximum fuel
Operational Equipment and Armament:
Weather and navigation/ground-mapping
radar in nose and undernose radomes.
APU makes aircraft independent of
ground facilities. Equipment for all-
weather day/night operation, including
automatic flight control and landing
approach. Two 23mm guns in manned
rear turret. ECM and flare dispensers.
Maximum payload 88,185lb (40,000kg).

MIL Mi-8 and Mi-17
NATO Reporting Name: 'Hip'
Armed assault transport, communications,
ECM and general-purpose helicopter
First flight: 1961
Estimated number operational in Soviet
forces: 2,500

An-12 (Cub)

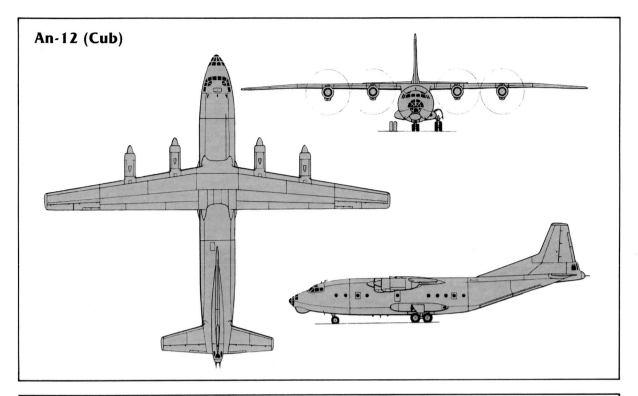

Il-76MD (Candid-B)

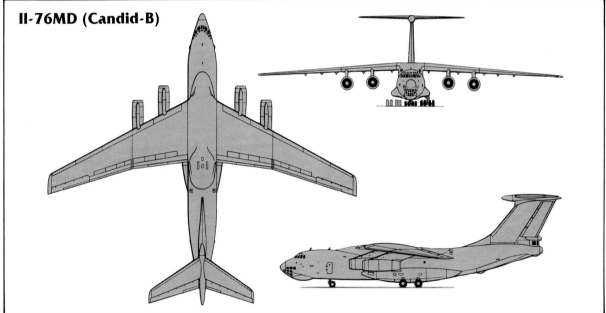

Variants

'Hip-C'. Basic version of Mi-8 to transport 24 fully equipped troops on tip-up seats along cabin sidewalls, or 8,820lb (4,000kg) of vehicles or freight. Can be adapted quickly to accommodate 12 stretcher patients and attendant. Loaded via rear clamshell doors and ramp, with a winch and pulley block system to facilitate freight handling. Twin racks on each side of cabin can carry a total of 128 rockets in four packs, or other weapons. Some uprated to Mi-17 standard as Mi-8Ts and Mi-8TBs.

'Hip-D'. Airborne communications version, with canisters on stores racks and added antennas.

'Hip-E'. As 'Hip-C', but with emphasis on

weapons for escort duties. One 12.7mm machine-gun in nose. Triple stores racks to carry total of 192 rockets plus four AT-2 'Swatter' anti-tank missiles. Some uprated to Mi-17 standard, with designation Mi-8TBK.

'Hip-G'. Airborne communications version with 'hockey stick' antennas.

'Hip-H'. Sole NATO designation for Mi-17, which is similar to Mi-8 but with Isotov TV3-117MT turboshaft engines (each 1,950shp; 1,454kW) in shorter housings, tail rotor on port side of vertical stabilizer. optional 23mm gun packs, and armour on the cockpit sides. Many Mi-8s have been converted to this standard.

'Hip-J'. ECM version of Mi-8, with small boxes on each side of fuselage, fore and

aft of undercarriage legs.

'Hip-K'. Another ECM version for communications jamming with an array of six dipole antennas on each side of cabin. Some uprated to Mi-17 standard, including Mi-17P version with new antenna array consisting of a large panel on each side.

Data for 'Hip-E'

Engines: Two Isotov TV2-117A turboshafts, each rated at 1,700shp (1,267kW). (Tail rotor on starboard side of vertical stabilizer.)

Main rotor diameter: 69ft 10¼in (21.29m)

Fuselage length excluding tail rotor: 59ft 7½in (18.17m)

Height: 18ft 6½in (5.65m)

Mi-8 (Hip)

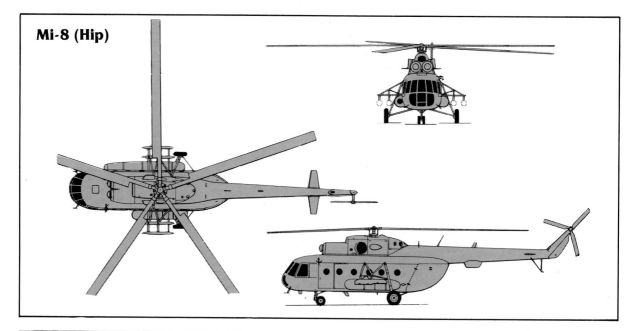

Mi-24 (Hind-D)

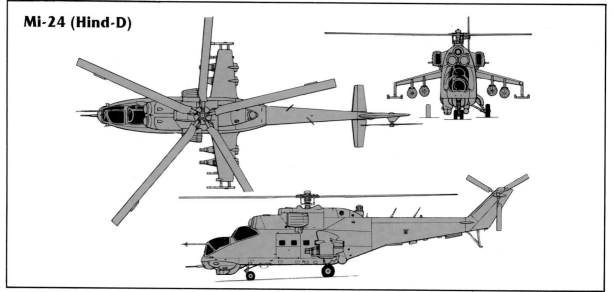

Maximum take-off weight: 26,455lb
(12,000kg)
Maximum cruising speed: 149mph
(240km/h)
Operational ceiling: 13,050ft (3,980m)
Maximum range: 307 miles (495km)
Operational Equipment and Armament: As
described under individual variant listings,
plus infra-red suppressor and flare
dispensers.

Picture notes
131. This Mi-8TBK is towing a target for
firing practice.
132. Casualty evacuation by an Mi-8 in
Arctic conditions.

MIL Mi-24
NATO Reporting Name: 'Hind'
Gunship helicopter, with transport
capability
First flight: Unknown
Estimated number operational in Soviet
forces: 1,250

Variants
'Hind-A, B and C'. Early versions. Designed
as armed transports for squad of eight
fully equipped assault troops. Crew of
three on large flight deck.
'Hind-D' (Mi-24D). Primary gunship. Front
fuselage redesigned above cabin floor to
house weapons operator and pilot in
separate cockpits, with flight mechanic in
main cabin. Troop carrying provisions
retained. Undernose Gatling-type
12.7mm four-barrel gun slaved to
adjacent electro-optical sight. Four pylons
under stub-wings for rocket packs (total
of 128 rockets), 20-round packs of larger
rockets, 23mm twin-barrel gun pods, up
to 3,300lb (1,500kg) of chemical or
conventional bombs, mine dispensers or
other stores. Four AT-2 ('Swatter') anti-
tank missiles on wingtip launchers, with RF
guidance pod under nose. IFF, radar
warning system, infra-red jammer and
flare dispensers.
'Hind-E' (Mi-24W). As Mi-24D, but revised
armament. Up to 12 AT-6 ('Spiral') tube-
launched anti-tank missiles on stub-wings.

Enlarged guidance pod. Able to carry
AA-8 ('Aphid') self-defence missiles.
'Hind-F' (Mi-24P). As Mi-24W, but nose
gun replaced by twin-barrel 30mm gun
on starboard side of front fuselage.
'Hind-G'. Basically as Mi-24W, but wingtip
endplate pylons carry 'clutching hand'
mechanisms associated with nuclear/
biological/chemical warfare.

Data for 'Hind-D'
Engines: Two Isotov TV3-117 turboshafts,
each rated at 2,200shp (1,640kW).
Main rotor diameter: 56ft 9in (17.30m)
Fuselage length excluding tail rotor and
gun: 57ft 5in (17.50m)
Height: 21ft 4in (6.50m)
Normal take-off weight: 24,250lb
(11,000kg)
Maximum level speed: 192mph (310km/h)
Operational ceiling: 14,750ft (4,500m)
Combat radius: 99 miles (160km) with
maximum military load
Operational Equipment and Armament: As
described under individual variant listings.

Mi-26 (Halo)

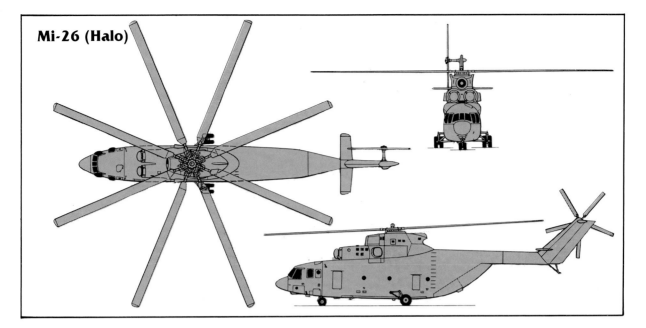

Ka-25 (Hormone-A)

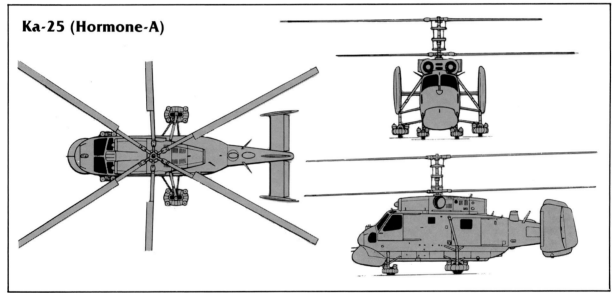

Picture notes
137. Lower aircraft is a 'Hind-G' with NBC
wingtip fittings.

MIL Mi-26
NATO Reporting Name: 'Halo'
Heavy-lift transport helicopter
First flight: 14 December 1977
Estimated number operational in Soviet
forces: more than 50

Variants
'Halo' (Mi-26). The only version known to
be operational. It is the heaviest
helicopter ever put into production, and
the first to have an eight-blade main rotor.
Normal configuration, as a freight
transport, provides for a crew of five on
the flight deck, with tip-up seats for about
20 passengers along walls of hold. Seats
can be installed for 85 combat-equipped
troops, plus four more passengers in
compartment aft of flight deck. Freight is
loaded via downward-hinged rear door
and folding ramp. Handling is facilitated

by two 5,511lb (2,500kg) overhead
hoists, an 1,100lb (500kg) winch and
roller conveyors. Typical freight loads
include two airborne infantry combat
vehicles or a standard 44,100lb
(20,000kg) ISO container. Payload is to
be increased to 48,500lb (22,000kg).

Data for 'Halo'
Engines: Two Lotarev D-136 turboshafts,
   each rated at 11,240shp (8,380kW).
Main rotor diameter: 105ft 0in (32.00m)
Fuselage length, excluding tail rotor: 110ft
   8in (33.727m)
Height: 26ft 8¾in (8.145m)
Maximum take-off weight: 123,450lb
   (56,000kg)
Maximum level speed: 183mph (295km/h)
Operational ceiling: 15,100ft (4,600m)
Maximum range: 497 miles (800km)
Operational Equipment and Armament: All
   items necessary for day and night
   operations in all weathers, including
   weather radar, Doppler navigation, map
   display and automatic hover capability.

Closed-circuit TV cameras to observe
slung loads. Infra-red jammers and
suppressors, chaff/flare dispensers, radar
warning receivers and colour-coded
identification flares on military 'Halos'. No
armament.

KAMOV Ka-25
NATO Reporting Name: 'Hormone'
Multi-role naval helicopter, with co-axial
contra-rotating rotors.
First flight: probably 1961
Estimated number operational with Soviet
Navy: 100

Variants
'Hormone-A' (Ka-25BSh). Anti-submarine
helicopter, with search radar in large, flat-
bottom housing under nose. Operational
on Soviet Navy carriers and from
platforms on a variety of other ships. Crew
of four or five. Can be fitted with folding
seats for up to 12 persons. Lack of
automatic hover capability precludes use
of sonar at night or in adverse weather.

Cylindrical canisters on each side of lower fuselage for markers, smoke generators or beacons.

'Hormone-B'. Equipped to acquire 'over-the-horizon' targets for missile launch crews on Soviet Navy ships. Larger nose radome with spherical undersurface. Data link equipment in small cylindrical radome under rear of cabin. Fuel in cylindrical canisters on each side of lower fuselage.

'Hormone-C'. Generally similar to 'Hormone-A', but equipped to provide midcourse guidance to long-range ship-launched surface-to-surface missiles. Yagi aerial on nose associated with guidance system. 'Hormone-C' is not required by newer missiles; so, many have had inessential operational equipment removed, and are used on utility and search and rescue duties.

Data for 'Hormone-A'
Engines: Two Glushenkov GTD-3BM turboshafts, each rated at 990shp (738kW).
Main rotor diameter (each): 51ft 7¾in (15.74m)

Fuselage length: 32ft 0in (9.75m)
Height: 17ft 7½in (5.37m)
Maximum take-off weight: 16,535lb (7,500kg)
Maximum level speed: 130mph (209km/h)
Operational ceiling: 11,000ft (3,350m)
Maximum range: 405 miles (650km)
Operational Equipment and Armament: Search radar under nose. Dipping sonar in compartment at rear of cabin. External canister of sonobuoys aft of starboard main landing gear. ESM 'flower pot' housing above tailboom. IFF and radar warning system. Two 18in (450mm) anti-submarine torpedoes, nuclear depth-charges and other stores in fuselage weapons bay.

BERIEV Be-12
NATO Reporting Name: 'Mail'
Anti-submarine and maritime patrol amphibian, in Soviet Navy service.
First flight: 1960
Estimated number operational with Soviet Navy: 75

Variants
'Mail' (Be-12, M-12). Only known version, with crew of five, serving from coastal bases of the Soviet Northern and Black Sea Fleets over a radius of around 230 miles (370km) from shore. Total of 100 built, from 1964. High-mounted engines, on cranked wings, keep propellers clear of spray during take-off and landing.

Data for 'Mail'
Engines: Two Ivchenko AI-20M turboprops, each rated at 4,190ehp (3,124kW).
Wing span: 97ft 5¾in (29.71m)
Length: 99ft 0in (30.17m)
Height: 22ft 11½in (7.00m)
Maximum take-off weight: 68,345lb (31,000kg)
Maximum level speed: 378mph (608km/h)
Operational ceiling: 37,000ft (11,280m)
Maximum range: 4,660 miles (7,500km)
Operational Equipment and Armament: Radar in nose, and magnetic anomaly detection (MAD) equipment in tail 'sting'. Internal stores bay in bottom of hull. Torpedoes, depth-charges, mines and other stores on four underwing pylons.

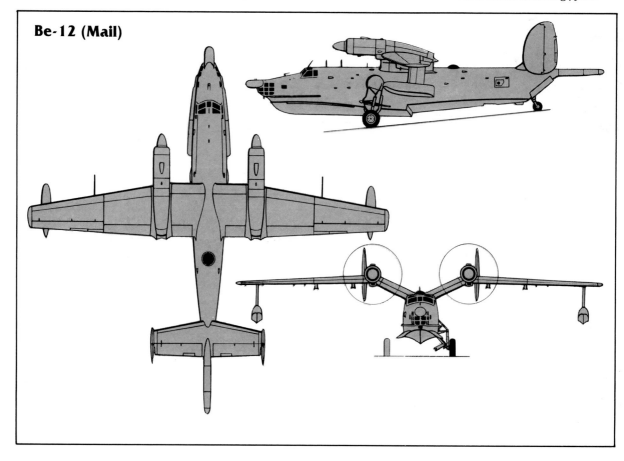

Be-12 (Mail)